HOW TO:

GENERATE PASSIVE INCOME

BY DWIGHT LEAD

I0489821

Welcome to "Unlocking Financial Freedom: Your Guide to Generating Passive Income in 2024." In today's fast-paced world, achieving financial independence is more important than ever. This book is designed to provide you with actionable strategies to build multiple streams of passive income, enabling you to enjoy financial security and the freedom to pursue your passions.

Dwight Lead

EMBRACING FINANCIAL FREEDOM

The pursuit of financial freedom is a goal shared by many, yet achieved by few. In a world where the cost of living continues to rise and job security is increasingly uncertain, the concept of generating passive income has never been more relevant. Imagine a life where your money works for you, creating streams of income that flow effortlessly into your bank account, allowing you to focus on what truly matters—whether it's spending time with loved ones, pursuing passions, or simply enjoying peace of mind.

Welcome to "Unlocking Financial Freedom: Your Guide to Generating Passive Income" This book is your roadmap to achieving the financial independence you've always dreamed of. Through proven strategies and modern opportunities, we will explore diverse methods to create passive income, enabling you to build a resilient financial future.

In the pages that follow, you'll discover the power of real estate crowdfunding, dividend stocks, online courses, and many other innovative avenues to generate passive income. Each chapter is designed to provide you with practical, actionable insights that you can implement immediately. You'll learn not only the theory behind these strategies but also step-by-step guides to get started and maximize your returns.

This book is not just about making money—it's about transforming your relationship with money. It's about breaking free from the constraints of the traditional 9-to-5 grind and designing a life that aligns with your values and aspirations. It's about creating a legacy of financial stability for yourself and your loved ones.

As you embark on this journey, remember that building passive income streams is not a get-rich-quick scheme. It requires patience, diligence, and a willingness to learn. But with commitment and the right strategies, financial freedom is within your reach.

So, are you ready to take the first step towards a life of abundance and security? Let's dive in and explore the exciting world of passive income opportunities. Your future self will thank you for the choices you make today.

1.

REAL ESTATE CROWD FUNDING

R eal estate has long been a popular investment avenue for those looking to generate passive income. However, the traditional route of purchasing and managing rental properties can be time-consuming and require substantial capital. Real estate crowdfunding presents a modern solution, allowing investors to pool their resources and invest in properties without the hassles of direct ownership. In this chapter, we will explore how real estate crowdfunding works, its benefits, and how you can get started.

- Real estate crowdfunding involves multiple investors pooling their money to invest in real estate projects. These projects can range from residential properties to commercial real estate developments. By leveraging the collective funds of many investors, crowdfunding platforms can provide access to high-value properties that might be out of reach for individual investors.

- Crowdfunding platforms act as intermediaries, connecting investors with real estate developers and property managers. These platforms vet the projects, ensuring they meet certain criteria before listing them for investment. This vetting process provides an added layer of security for investors, although it's important to conduct your own due diligence as well.

"UNLOCK FINANCIAL FREEDOM BY LETTING YOUR MONEY WORK FOR YOU THROUGH REAL ESTATE CROWDFUNDING—WHERE COLLECTIVE INVESTMENT MEETS EFFORTLESS PASSIVE INCOME."

BENEFITS OF REAL ESTATE CROWDFUNDING

1. Lower Entry Barriers: One of the primary advantages of real estate crowdfunding is the lower capital requirement. Unlike traditional real estate investments, which often require significant upfront capital, crowdfunding allows you to start with a much smaller investment.

2. Diversification: Crowdfunding enables you to spread your investment across multiple properties and locations, reducing the risk associated with investing in a single property.

3. Passive Income: Once you've made your investment, the income generated from the property—whether through rental income or profits from property sales—flows to you without requiring active management.

4. Access to Premium Properties: By pooling resources with other investors, you can gain access to high-quality properties and commercial developments that would be otherwise unattainable.

5. Professional Management: Properties are managed by experienced real estate professionals, ensuring that they are well-maintained and rented out efficiently.

HOW TO GET STARTED

1. Choose a Crowdfunding Platform: The first step is to select a reputable real estate crowdfunding platform. Some of the well-known platforms include Fundrise, RealtyMogul, and Crowdstreet. Research each platform's offerings, fees, and track record to find the one that best suits your investment goals.

2. Create an Account: Once you've chosen a platform, you'll need to create an account. This typically involves providing personal information and completing a verification process.

3. Explore Investment Opportunities: After setting up your account, browse the available investment opportunities. Each listing will provide detailed information about the property, the investment terms, projected returns, and the minimum investment required.

4. Conduct Due Diligence: Before investing, it's crucial to conduct your own research. Review the property details, the track record of the developers, and the financial projections. Make sure the investment aligns with your risk tolerance and financial goals.

5. Invest: Once you've identified a suitable opportunity, you can proceed with your investment. Most platforms allow you to invest directly through their website, making the process straightforward.

6. Monitor Your Investment: After investing, you can track the performance of your investment through the platform's dashboard. You'll receive regular updates on the property's status and financial performance.

7. Reinvest Earnings: As you begin to receive returns from your investment, consider reinvesting them into new opportunities to compound your earnings and grow your passive income stream.

TIPS FOR SUCCESS

❖ - Start Small: Begin with a small investment to familiarize yourself with the process and the platform.
❖ - Diversify: Spread your investments across different properties and types of real estate to mitigate risk.
❖ - Stay Informed: Keep up-to-date with real estate market trends and platform updates to make informed investment decisions.
❖ - Review Fees: Be aware of any fees associated with the platform, as these can impact your overall returns.

CONCLUSION

Real estate crowdfunding offers an accessible and effective way to generate passive income. By leveraging the power of collective investment, you can enjoy the benefits of real estate ownership without the associated hassles. With careful research and strategic investments, real estate crowdfunding can be a valuable addition to your passive income portfolio.

2.
DIVIDEND STOCKS

Dividend stocks offer a powerful way to generate passive income, providing regular payouts from the profits of established companies. By investing in dividend-paying stocks, you can create a steady stream of income without the need to sell your shares. This chapter will guide you through the basics of dividend stocks, how to select the right ones, and strategies to maximize your returns.

- Dividend stocks are shares of companies that return a portion of their earnings to shareholders regularly, typically on a quarterly basis. These payouts, known as dividends, can be an attractive source of passive income. Companies that pay dividends are usually well-established with stable earnings, making them less volatile than growth stocks.

- There are two primary types of dividends:

Cash Dividends: The most common form, where shareholders receive a cash payment per share owned.

Stock Dividends: Instead of cash, shareholders receive additional shares, increasing their holdings in the company.

"UNLOCK STEADY, GROWING WEALTH BY INVESTING IN DIVIDEND STOCKS— WHERE YOUR MONEY WORKS AND GROWS FOR YOU, EFFORTLESSLY."

BENEFITS OF DIVIDEND STOCK

1.Regular Income: Dividends provide a consistent income stream, which can be reinvested or used to cover living expenses.

2.Capital Appreciation: Besides dividends, the value of your stocks can increase over time, adding to your overall returns.

3. Lower Volatility: Dividend-paying companies are often more stable, making their stocks less susceptible to market fluctuations.

4. Inflation Hedge: Dividend growth can outpace inflation, preserving your purchasing power.

HOW TO GET STARTED

1. Research Dividend Stocks: Begin by researching companies with a strong track record of paying and increasing dividends. Look for companies with stable earnings, solid cash flow, and a commitment to returning capital to shareholders.

2. Dividend Yield: This is the annual dividend payment divided by the stock's current price. A higher yield indicates a higher return on investment, but it's essential to consider the company's financial health. Extremely high yields can sometimes be a red flag, indicating potential financial distress.

3. Payout Ratio: This ratio measures the proportion of earnings paid out as dividends. A lower payout ratio suggests that the company retains enough earnings to reinvest in its growth, making it more likely to sustain its dividend payments.

4. Dividend Growth Ratio: Companies that consistently increase their dividends over time are often better long-term investments. This growth demonstrates financial health and a commitment to rewarding shareholders.

5. Create a Diversified Portfolio: Diversify your investments across various sectors to mitigate risk. Different industries perform differently under various economic conditions, so spreading your investments helps protect against sector-specific downturns.

6. Use Dividend Reinvestment Plans (DRIPs): Many companies offer DRIPs, allowing you to reinvest your dividends to purchase additional shares automatically. This compounding effect can significantly boost your investment over time.

7. Monitor and Adjust: Keep an eye on your portfolio's performance and the companies you've invested in. Be prepared to adjust your holdings if a company's financial health declines or if better opportunities arise.

Let's walk through an example of building a dividend stock portfolio. Suppose you have $10,000 to invest. Here's a step-by-step approach:

1. Select Blue-Chip Stocks: Choose established companies with a strong dividend history, such as Johnson & Johnson, Procter & Gamble, and Coca-Cola. These companies offer stability and consistent dividends.

2. Allocate Funds: Spread your investment across these companies. For instance, invest $2,000 in each of five different stocks.

3. Reinvest Dividends: Enroll in DRIPs to reinvest dividends automatically, buying more shares and compounding your returns.

4. Monitor Performance: Regularly review your portfolio and stay updated on the companies' financial health. Make adjustments as necessary to optimize your returns.

TIPS FOR SUCCESS

❖ - Start with Research: Utilize resources like financial news websites, investment platforms, and company annual reports to research potential investments.
❖ - Focus on Quality: Prioritize companies with a solid track record of dividend payments and financial stability.
❖ - Stay Patient: Dividend investing is a long-term strategy. Reinvesting dividends and allowing your investments to grow over time will yield the best results.
❖ - Seek Professional Advice: Consider consulting a financial advisor to tailor a dividend investment strategy that aligns with your financial goals and risk tolerance..

CONCLUSION

Investing in dividend stocks is a proven method to generate passive income while benefiting from the potential for capital appreciation. By selecting high-quality dividend-paying companies, diversifying your portfolio, and reinvesting dividends, you can build a reliable income stream that grows over time. Embrace the power of dividend investing and take a significant step towards achieving financial freedom.

3.
PEER TO PEER LENDING

eer-to-peer (P2P) lending has emerged as a compelling way to generate passive income, allowing individuals to lend money directly to borrowers and earn interest on their loans. This innovative approach to lending bypasses traditional financial institutions, offering attractive returns for lenders and accessible credit for borrowers. In this chapter, we will delve into the mechanics of P2P lending, its benefits, and how you can effectively get started.Real estate crowdfunding involves multiple investors pooling their money to invest in real estate projects. These projects can range from residential properties to commercial real estate developments. By leveraging the collective funds of many investors, crowdfunding platforms can provide access to high-value properties that might be out of reach for individual investors.

- Peer-to-peer lending platforms connect lenders with borrowers, facilitating loans for various purposes such as personal loans, business financing, and debt consolidation. By investing in these loans, you become the lender, earning interest payments over time. The P2P platforms handle the logistics of loan origination, servicing, and collections, making it a relatively hands-off investment for you."Unlock financial freedom by letting your money work for you through real estate crowdfunding—where collective investment meets effortless passive income."

"THE P2P PLATFORMS HANDLE THE LOGISTICS OF LOAN ORIGINATION, SERVICING, AND COLLECTIONS, MAKING IT A RELATIVELY HANDS-OFF INVESTMENT FOR YOU."

BENEFITS OF PEER-TO-PEER LENDING

1. High Returns: P2P lending can offer higher returns compared to traditional savings accounts or bonds, making it an attractive option for income-focused investors.

2. Diversification: Investing in a range of loans allows you to diversify your portfolio, spreading risk across multiple borrowers and reducing the impact of any single default.

3. Accessibility: P2P platforms typically have lower minimum investment requirements, making it easy to start with a small amount of capital.

4. Monthly Cash Flow: As borrowers make monthly payments, you receive regular income, which can be reinvested or withdrawn as needed..

HOW TO GET STARTED

1. Choose a P2P Lending Platform: Select a reputable P2P lending platform. Some well-known options include LendingClub, Prosper, and Funding Circle. Research each

platform's loan offerings, fees, and borrower profiles to find one that aligns with your investment goals.

2. Create an Account: Sign up on your chosen platform, providing necessary personal information and completing the verification process.

3. Fund Your Account: Deposit funds into your account. The minimum investment can vary by platform, but it is typically quite accessible.

4. Explore Loan Listings: Browse the available loan listings on the platform. Each listing includes details about the borrower, the loan purpose, the interest rate, and the risk grade assigned by the platform.

5. Diversify Your Investments: To mitigate risk, spread your investment across multiple loans. For example, if you have $5,000 to invest, consider funding 50 different loans with $100 each.

6. Monitor Performance: Regularly review your loan portfolio's performance through the platform's dashboard. Track the status of your loans, interest payments, and any defaults.

7. Reinvest Earnings: As you receive interest payments, reinvest them into new loans to compound your returns and grow your passive income stream. ####

Let's walk through an example of building a P2P lending portfolio. Suppose you have $10,000 to invest. Here's a step-by-step approach:

1. Select a Platform: Choose LendingClub for its user-friendly interface and diverse loan offerings.

2. Create an Account: Sign up and deposit $10,000 into your account.

3. Diversify Investments: Invest in 100 different loans, allocating $100 to each. Choose loans with varying risk grades to balance potential returns and risk.

4. Monitor and Reinvest: Track the performance of your loans. Reinvest the interest payments you receive into new loans to maximize your returns.

Managing Risk in P2P Lending

While P2P lending can offer high returns, it also comes with risks, primarily the risk of borrower default. Here are some strategies to manage this risk:

- Diversification: Spread your investments across a large number of loans to reduce the impact of any single default.
- Loan Grades: Invest in loans with different risk grades. Higher-grade loans typically offer lower returns but come with less risk, while lower-grade loans can offer higher returns but carry more risk.
- Regular Monitoring: Keep an eye on your portfolio's performance and be prepared to adjust your strategy if default rates rise.

TIPS FOR SUCCESS

❖ - Start Small: Begin with a small investment to understand how the platform works and how loans perform.
❖ - Automate Investing: Use automated investment tools offered by many platforms to quickly

CONCLUSION

Peer-to-peer lending presents a dynamic and accessible avenue for generating passive income. By leveraging modern technology to connect directly with borrowers, you can enjoy the benefits of high returns, diversified investments, and regular cash flow. While the potential for default exists, prudent strategies such as diversifying across numerous loans and balancing risk grades can help mitigate this risk.

Embarking on a P2P lending journey allows you to be more than just an investor—you become a vital part of the financial ecosystem, providing much-needed credit to individuals and businesses. With careful planning, diligent monitoring, and strategic reinvestment, peer-to-peer lending can become a cornerstone of your passive income portfolio, helping you move closer to financial freedom.

As you continue to explore and expand your investment strategies, remember that success in P2P lending, like any investment, requires patience, research, and adaptability. By following the guidelines and tips outlined in this chapter, you are well on your way to harnessing the power of peer-to-peer lending to build a robust and rewarding passive income stream.

4.
CREATE AN ONLINE COURSE

The digital age has revolutionized the way we learn and share knowledge. Creating an online course offers a fantastic opportunity to generate passive income by leveraging your expertise and reaching a global audience. Whether you're an expert in a professional field, a hobbyist with specialized skills, or a passionate teacher, an online course can turn your knowledge into a lucrative income stream. In this chapter, we'll explore the steps to create, launch, and monetize an online course effectively.Real estate crowdfunding involves multiple investors pooling their money to invest in real estate projects. These projects can range from residential properties to commercial real estate developments. By leveraging the collective funds of many investors, crowdfunding platforms can provide access to high-value properties that might be out of reach for individual investors.

- An online course is a structured program of learning delivered over the internet. It can consist of video lectures, written content, quizzes, and interactive assignments. Platforms like Udemy, Teachable, and Coursera have made it easier than ever to create and distribute online courses to a wide audience"Unlock financial freedom by letting your money work for you through real estate crowdfunding —where collective investment meets effortless passive income."

"TRANSFORM YOUR EXPERTISE INTO A GLOBAL INCOME STREAM—CREATE AN ONLINE COURSE AND WATCH YOUR KNOWLEDGE GENERATE PASSIVE INCOME EFFORTLESSLY."

BENEFITS OF CREATING AN ONLINE COURSE

1. Scalability: Once created, an online course can be sold to an unlimited number of students, providing ongoing income without additional effort.
2. Flexibility: You can create a course on virtually any topic, tailored to your expertise and interests.
3. Global Reach: Online platforms allow you to reach a global audience, expanding your potential market exponentially.
4. Low Overhead: Compared to traditional teaching, creating an online course requires minimal investment in materials and infrastructure.

HOW TO GET STARTED

1. Identify Your Niche: Choose a topic you are knowledgeable and passionate about. Ensure there is demand for this topic by researching online learning platforms, forums, and social media to see what potential students are interested in learning.

2. Define Your Audience: Understand who your target students are. What are their needs, goals, and challenges? This will help you tailor your content to meet their specific needs.

3. Create a Course Outline: Plan your course structure. Break down your topic into modules and lessons, creating a logical flow of information. Each module should cover a specific aspect of the topic in detail.

4. Develop Course Content: Start creating your course content. This can include video lectures, written guides, slideshows, quizzes, and interactive assignments. Use high-quality audio and video equipment to ensure your course is professional and engaging.

5. Choose a Platform: Select an online course platform to host and sell your course. Platforms like Udemy and Teachable offer robust tools for course creation, marketing, and sales. Evaluate their features, fees, and audience reach to choose the best fit for your course.

6. Set Your Price: Decide on a pricing strategy. Consider factors like course length, depth of content, and market competition. You can offer tiered pricing with different levels of access and additional resources for higher tiers.

7. Launch Your Course: Once your course is ready, launch it on your chosen platform. Leverage your network, social media, and email marketing to promote your course and attract students.

8. Engage with Students: Although the course itself is passive, engaging with your students through Q&A sessions, discussion forums, and feedback can enhance their experience and encourage positive reviews and referrals.

9. Collect Feedback and Improve: Gather feedback from your students to identify areas for improvement. Regularly update your course content to keep it relevant and valuable.

Let's walk through an example of creating a successful online course. Suppose you are a digital marketing expert. Here's a step-by-step approach:

1. Identify Your Niche: Choose a specific aspect of digital marketing, such as "SEO for Beginners."

2. Define Your Audience: Target small business owners and aspiring digital marketers who want to learn SEO basics.

3. Create a Course Outline: Plan modules like Introduction to SEO, Keyword Research, On-Page SEO, Off-Page SEO, and Measuring SEO Success.

4. Develop Course Content: Record video lectures for each module, create downloadable resources like cheat sheets and templates, and include quizzes to reinforce learning.

5. Choose a Platform: Opt for Teachable for its user-friendly interface and strong marketing tools.

6. Set Your Price: Price your course at $199, with an option for a premium package at $299, including one-on-one coaching sessions.

7. Launch Your Course: Promote your course through your blog, social media channels, and email list. Offer a limited-time discount to generate initial interest and enrollments.

8. Engage with Students: Host monthly live Q&A sessions to address student questions and provide additional value.

9. Collect Feedback and Improve: Use student feedback to refine your content, add new modules on emerging SEO trends, and update existing lessons with the latest information.

TIPS FOR SUCCESS

❖ - Focus on Quality: Invest in good equipment and take the time to create high-quality content that stands out.
❖ - Be Consistent: Regularly update your course to keep it current and valuable.
❖ - Leverage Marketing: Use various marketing strategies, including social media, email marketing, and partnerships, to reach a broader audience.
❖ -Engage with Your Audience: Building a community around your course can increase engagement and lead to more referrals and repeat customers.

CONCLUSION

Creating an online course is a powerful way to generate passive income while sharing your expertise with a global audience. By carefully planning your course, choosing the right platform, and engaging with your students, you can build a sustainable income stream that grows over time. Embrace the potential of online education, and turn your knowledge into a profitable venture that benefits both you and your learners.

5.
CREATE AN E-BOOK

Writing an e-book is an excellent way to generate passive income, leveraging your knowledge, creativity, and passion to create a digital product that can be sold indefinitely. Whether you have expertise in a particular field, a compelling story to tell, or valuable insights to share, an e-book allows you to reach a global audience and generate ongoing revenue. In this chapter, we will explore the steps to write, publish, and market an e-book effectively.Real estate crowdfunding involves multiple investors pooling their money to invest in real estate projects. These projects can range from residential properties to commercial real estate developments. By leveraging the collective funds of many investors, crowdfunding platforms can provide access to high-value properties that might be out of reach for individual investors.

- An e-book (electronic book) is a digital version of a book that can be read on computers, e-readers, tablets, and smartphones. The popularity of e-books has surged due to their convenience, accessibility, and the growing trend of digital consumption. Platforms like Amazon Kindle Direct Publishing (KDP), Apple Books, and Smashwords have made it easier than ever to publish and distribute e-books to a wide audience.

"TRANSFORM YOUR KNOWLEDGE INTO AN EVERGREEN REVENUE STREAM— WRITE AN E-BOOK AND EARN PASSIVE INCOME FOR YEARS TO COME."

BENEFITS OF WRITING AN E-BOOK

1. Low Production Costs: Unlike traditional publishing, e-books have minimal production costs, allowing for higher profit margins.

2. Global Reach: Digital platforms enable your e-book to be accessible to readers worldwide.

3. Scalability: Once written, an e-book can be sold repeatedly without additional effort, generating ongoing passive income.

4. Creative Control: Self-publishing gives you complete control over the content, design, and pricing of your e-book.

HOW TO GET STARTED

1. Choose Your Topic: Select a topic you are knowledgeable about and passionate about. Ensure there is demand for this topic by researching what readers are looking for in your niche. Browse bestsellers in your genre and identify gaps or areas where you can provide unique value.

2. Define Your Audience: Understand who your target readers are. Consider their needs, interests, and pain points. Tailor your content to address these aspects effectively.

3. Outline Your E-book: Create a detailed outline to organize your thoughts and structure your e-book. Break down your topic into chapters or sections, creating a logical flow of information. An outline will serve as a roadmap, keeping you focused and on track during the writing process.

4. Write Your E-book: Begin writing your e-book based on your outline. Focus on delivering valuable content in a clear, engaging, and concise manner. Use a conversational tone to connect with your readers and make the material accessible.

5. Edit and Proofread: Once your first draft is complete, thoroughly edit and proofread your e-book. Consider hiring a professional editor or using tools like Grammarly to ensure your writing is polished and error-free.

6. Design a Professional Cover: A compelling cover is crucial for attracting readers. Invest in a professionally designed cover that reflects the theme and quality of your e-book. Platforms like Canva or services from professional designers can help you create an eye-catching cover.

7. Format Your E-book: Proper formatting ensures your e-book is readable on various devices. Use formatting tools or services that cater to e-book publishing standards. Amazon KDP, for example, offers guidelines and tools for formatting.

8. Publish Your E-book: Choose a self-publishing platform to publish your e-book. Amazon KDP is a popular choice, offering a vast audience and various marketing tools. Follow the platform's guidelines to upload your e-book, set your price, and publish it.

9. Market Your E-book: Effective marketing is key to generating sales. Utilize social media, email marketing, and your website to promote your e-book. Consider running promotional campaigns or using Amazon's advertising services to increase visibility.

10. Gather Reviews and Feedback: Encourage readers to leave reviews and provide feedback. Positive reviews enhance credibility and attract more readers. Use feedback to improve future editions or new projects.

Let's walk through an example of writing and publishing an e-book. Suppose you have expertise in personal finance. Here's a step-by-step approach:

1. Choose Your Topic: Select "Smart Budgeting for Millennials" as your e-book topic.
2. Define Your Audience: Target millennials who are looking to manage their finances better.
3. Outline Your E-book: Plan chapters such as Introduction to Budgeting, Tracking Expenses, Saving Strategies, and Debt Management.
4. Write Your E-book: Write engaging content, providing practical tips, examples, and case studies.
5. Edit and Proofread: Hire a professional editor to polish your manuscript.
6. Design a Professional Cover: Use a platform like Canva to design a visually appealing cover.

TIPS FOR SUCCESS

❖ Research Thoroughly: Understand your market and audience to create content that resonates.

❖ Maintain Consistency: Write regularly to keep the momentum going and meet your deadlines.

❖ Leverage Multiple Platforms: Publish on various platforms to reach a broader audience.

❖ Build an Author Platform: Establish your presence on social media, start a blog, or create a website to connect with your audience and promote your e-book.

❖ Use Keywords: Optimize your e-book's title and description with relevant keywords to improve discoverability on search engines and e-book platforms.

CONCLUSION

Writing an e-book is a powerful way to share your knowledge, reach a global audience, and generate passive income. With careful planning, quality content, and effective marketing, your e-book can become a valuable asset that provides ongoing revenue. Embrace the creative process, leverage digital platforms, and turn your ideas into a successful e-book that resonates with readers and boosts your financial independence.

6.
INVEST IN REIT'S

R eal Estate Investment Trusts (REITs) offer a compelling way to invest in real estate and generate passive income without the need to directly own or manage properties. By purchasing shares in REITs, you can benefit from the income generated by a diversified portfolio of real estate assets. In this chapter, we will explore what REITs are, the advantages of investing in them, and how to get started.Real estate crowdfunding involves multiple investors pooling their money to invest in real estate projects. These projects can range from residential properties to commercial real estate developments. By leveraging the collective funds of many investors, crowdfunding platforms can provide access to high-value properties that might be out of reach for individual investors.

- A Real Estate Investment Trust (REIT) is a company that owns, operates, or finances income-producing real estate. REITs pool capital from numerous investors to purchase and manage a portfolio of properties or real estate loans. They are required by law to distribute at least 90% of their taxable income to shareholders in the form of dividends, making them an attractive option for generating passive income."Unlock financial freedom by letting your money work for you through real estate crowdfunding—where collective investment meets effortless passive income."
- There are several types of REITs:

1. Equity REITs: These REITs own and operate income-producing real estate, such as office buildings, shopping malls, and apartment complexes.
2. Mortgage REITs (mREITs): These REITs provide financing for income-producing real estate by purchasing or originating mortgages and mortgage-backed securities.
3. Hybrid REITs: These REITs combine the investment strategies of both equity REITs and mortgage REITs.

BENEFITS OF REIT'S

1. Regular Income: REITs are required to pay out most of their income as dividends, providing a steady stream of passive income.
2. Diversification: Investing in REITs allows you to diversify your portfolio with exposure to real estate without the need to directly own property.
3. Liquidity: Unlike physical real estate, REIT shares can be bought and sold easily on major stock exchanges, providing liquidity to investors.
4. Professional Management: REITs are managed by experienced professionals who handle property acquisition, management, and leasing, reducing the burden on individual investors.
5. Accessibility: REITs offer an affordable way to invest in high-quality commercial real estate that might be out of reach for individual investors.

HOW TO GET STARTED

1. Research REITs: Start by researching different REITs to understand their investment focus, property portfolio, and

performance. Look for REITs with a strong track record, high occupancy rates, and sustainable dividend payouts. Resources like NAREIT (National Association of Real Estate Investment Trusts) and financial news websites can provide valuable insights.

2. Determine Your Investment Strategy: Decide whether you want to invest in equity REITs, mortgage REITs, or a combination of both. Equity REITs tend to be less volatile and provide steady income, while mortgage REITs can offer higher yields but come with greater risk.

3. Open a Brokerage Account: To invest in REITs, you'll need a brokerage account. Choose a reputable brokerage that offers a wide range of REITs and provides research tools to help you make informed decisions.

4. Evaluate REIT Performance: Assess the performance of potential REIT investments by examining key metrics such as dividend yield, funds from operations (FFO), and net asset value (NAV). Compare these metrics across different REITs to identify the best options for your portfolio.

5. Diversify Your REIT Holdings: Diversify your investments by selecting REITs with exposure to different types of properties and geographical locations. This can help mitigate risks associated with specific sectors or regions.

6. Monitor Your Investments: Regularly review the performance of your REIT investments and stay informed about market trends and economic conditions that could impact the real estate sector. Adjust your portfolio as needed to optimize returns.

Let's walk through an example of building a REIT portfolio. Suppose you have $10,000 to invest. Here's a step-by-step approach:

1. Research and Select REITs: Identify three REITs with strong performance and diversified property portfolios: a retail REIT, a healthcare REIT, and a residential REIT.

2. Open a Brokerage Account: Set up an account with a brokerage that offers access to these REITs.

3. Allocate Funds: Invest $3,000 in each of the three selected REITs and keep $1,000 as cash reserve for future opportunities.

4. Evaluate Performance: Monitor the performance of your REITs by reviewing quarterly reports and dividend payments.

5. Reinvest Dividends: Use the dividends you receive to reinvest in additional REIT shares, compounding your returns over time.

TIPS FOR SUCCESS

❖ Research Thoroughly: Conduct thorough research before investing in any REIT to ensure it aligns with your investment goals and risk tolerance.

❖ Focus on Quality: Choose REITs with high-quality assets and strong management teams.

❖ Diversify: Spread your investments across different REIT sectors to reduce risk.

❖ Stay Informed: Keep up-to-date with market trends, economic indicators, and changes in real estate regulations that could impact your investments.

❖ Reinvest Dividends: Consider reinvesting your dividends to take advantage of compounding growth.

CONCLUSION

Investing in REITs is a practical and efficient way to generate passive income through real estate without the complexities of property ownership. By carefully selecting high-quality REITs, diversifying your portfolio, and regularly monitoring your investments, you can enjoy the benefits of real estate income and capital appreciation. Embrace the potential of REITs to build a reliable and sustainable passive income stream, contributing to your financial independence and long-term wealth growth..

7.
AFFILIATE MARKETING

Affiliate marketing is a powerful and accessible way to generate passive income by promoting products or services and earning commissions on sales made through your referral links. It leverages the power of the internet and digital marketing to create a revenue stream with minimal upfront investment. This chapter will guide you through the basics of affiliate marketing, how to get started, and strategies to maximize your earnings.Real estate crowdfunding involves multiple investors pooling their money to invest in real estate projects. These projects can range from residential properties to commercial real estate developments. By leveraging the collective funds of many investors, crowdfunding platforms can provide access to high-value properties that might be out of reach for individual investors.

- Affiliate marketing involves partnering with companies to promote their products or services through unique referral links. When someone clicks on your link and makes a purchase, you earn a commission. This can be done through various online platforms, including blogs, social media, email newsletters, and websites.

"TURN YOUR PASSION INTO PROFIT WITH AFFILIATE MARKETING—EARN PASSIVE INCOME BY SHARING PRODUCTS YOU LOVE."

BENEFITS OF AFFILIATE MARKETING

1. Low Startup Costs: Affiliate marketing requires little to no upfront investment. You don't need to create products or maintain inventory.

2. Passive Income Potential: Once you've set up your affiliate links and content, you can earn money continuously as long as people make purchases through your links.

3. Flexibility: You can promote a wide range of products or services from various industries, allowing you to choose what aligns best with your interests and audience.

4. Scalability: As your online presence grows, so can your affiliate marketing income. There's no limit to how many products you can promote or how many sales you can make.

HOW TO GET STARTED

1. Choose a Niche: Select a specific area of interest or expertise that you are passionate about. A focused niche

helps you attract a targeted audience and become a trusted source of information.

2. Research Affiliate Programs: Look for reputable affiliate programs that offer products or services relevant to your niche. Popular platforms include Amazon Associates, ClickBank, ShareASale, and CJ Affiliate. Evaluate the commission rates, cookie duration, and payment terms.

3. Build a Platform: Create a platform to promote your affiliate links. This could be a blog, YouTube channel, social media profiles, or an email newsletter. Choose a platform where your target audience is most active and engaged.

4. Create Quality Content: Develop valuable content that incorporates your affiliate links naturally. This can include product reviews, how-to guides, tutorials, listicles, and personal recommendations. Ensure your content is informative, engaging, and helpful to your audience.

5. Incorporate SEO Strategies: Optimize your content for search engines to increase visibility and attract organic traffic. Use relevant keywords, create high-quality backlinks, and ensure your website is mobile-friendly.

6. Promote Your Content: Share your content across various channels to reach a wider audience. Use social media, email marketing, and online communities to drive traffic to your platform. Engage with your audience and encourage them to share your content.

7. Monitor Performance: Use analytics tools to track the performance of your affiliate links and content. Analyze metrics such as click-through rates, conversion rates, and total sales to identify what's working and where improvements can be made.

8. Optimize and Scale: Continuously optimize your content and strategies based on performance data. Experiment with different types of content, promotional tactics, and affiliate programs to maximize your earnings. As your audience grows, scale up your efforts to increase your passive income.

Let's walk through an example of building an affiliate marketing strategy. Suppose you are passionate about fitness and wellness. Here's a step-by-step approach:

    1. Choose a Niche: Focus on "home fitness for busy professionals."

    2. Research Affiliate Programs: Join affiliate programs from fitness equipment brands, health supplement companies, and online fitness courses.

    3. Build a Platform: Create a blog and a YouTube channel where you share fitness tips, workout routines, and product reviews.

    4. Create Quality Content: Write blog posts like "Top 10 Home Gym Essentials" and create videos demonstrating the use of fitness equipment, including your affiliate links.

    5. Incorporate SEO Strategies: Optimize your blog posts and video descriptions with keywords like "home fitness," "best workout equipment," and "fitness for busy professionals."

    6. Promote Your Content: Share your blog posts and videos on social media platforms, fitness forums, and email newsletters to drive traffic.

    7. Monitor Performance: Use tools like Google Analytics and the affiliate program's dashboard to track clicks, conversions, and earnings.

    8. Optimize and Scale: Identify which content performs best and create more of it. Experiment with different types of promotions, such as fitness challenges or discount codes, to boost engagement and sales.

TIPS FOR SUCCESS

❖ Be Authentic: Only promote products and services you genuinely believe in. Your audience will trust your recommendations more if they feel your endorsements are sincere.

❖ Engage with Your Audience: Build a relationship with your audience by responding to comments, answering questions, and providing additional value.

❖ Stay Updated: Keep up with the latest trends and updates in your niche to ensure your content remains relevant and valuable.

❖ Diversify Income Streams: Don't rely on a single affiliate program or product. Diversify your promotions to reduce risk and increase earning potential.

❖ Be Patient: Affiliate marketing takes time to build momentum. Consistent effort and high-quality content will pay off in the long run.

CONCLUSION

Affiliate marketing is a versatile and scalable way to generate passive income by leveraging your online presence. By choosing the right niche, creating valuable content, and promoting relevant products, you can build a sustainable income stream that grows with your audience. Embrace the potential of affiliate marketing to turn your passions and expertise into a profitable venture, contributing to your financial independence and long-term success.

8.
CREATE A MOBILE APP

The mobile app industry has experienced explosive growth over the past decade, providing numerous opportunities to generate passive income. By creating and monetizing a mobile app, you can reach millions of users worldwide and earn money continuously. Whether you have a unique app idea, a solution to a common problem, or a game concept, developing a mobile app can be a lucrative venture. In this chapter, we will explore the steps to create, launch, and monetize a mobile app effectively. Real estate crowdfunding involves multiple investors pooling their money to invest in real estate projects. These projects can range from residential properties to commercial real estate developments. By leveraging the collective funds of many investors, crowdfunding platforms can provide access to high-value properties that might be out of reach for individual investors.

- A mobile app is a software application designed to run on smartphones, tablets, and other mobile devices. Apps can serve various purposes, including entertainment, productivity, social networking, and education. The key to generating passive income through a mobile app lies in its monetization strategy, user engagement, and scalability.

"TURN YOUR APP IDEA INTO A GLOBAL INCOME STREAM—CREATE, LAUNCH, AND MONETIZE A MOBILE APP FOR ENDLESS PASSIVE INCOME."

BENEFITS OF CREATING A MOBILE APP

1. Global Reach: Mobile apps can reach a vast audience, with billions of smartphone users worldwide.

2. Scalability: Once developed, a mobile app can be distributed to an unlimited number of users, providing ongoing income without additional effort.

3. Diverse Monetization Options: There are multiple ways to monetize a mobile app, including in-app purchases, advertisements, subscriptions, and paid downloads.

4. Low Operating Costs: After the initial development, maintaining and updating an app typically involves lower costs compared to traditional businesses.

HOW TO GET STARTED

1. Identify Your App Idea: Start with a clear and compelling app idea. It should address a specific need, solve a problem, or provide entertainment. Conduct market research to validate your idea, identify your target audience, and analyze competitors.

2. Plan Your App: Create a detailed plan outlining the app's features, user interface, and user experience. Sketch wireframes and design mockups to visualize the app's layout and functionality. Consider the platforms (iOS, Android, or both) on which you want to launch your app.

3. Choose a Development Approach: Decide whether to develop the app yourself or hire a professional developer. If you have programming skills, you can use app development tools like Xcode for iOS or Android Studio for Android. Alternatively, you can hire freelance developers or a development agency to bring your idea to life.

4. Develop Your App: Start the development process by coding the app's core features and functionality. Ensure the app is user-friendly, visually appealing, and performs well on various devices. Test the app thoroughly to identify and fix any bugs or issues.

5. Implement Monetization Strategies: Choose the best monetization methods for your app:
   - In-App Purchases: Offer additional features, virtual goods, or premium content for a fee.
   - Advertisements: Display ads within your app using ad networks like Google AdMob or Facebook Audience Network.
   - Subscriptions: Charge users a recurring fee for access to premium features or content.
   - Paid Downloads: Charge users a one-time fee to download your app from app stores.

6. Launch Your App: Publish your app on app stores like Apple's App Store and Google Play Store. Follow the submission guidelines, create an appealing app description, and use high-quality screenshots and videos to attract users.

7. Promote Your App: Use various marketing strategies to increase visibility and downloads. Utilize social media, app

review websites, and influencer partnerships to spread the word. Consider running paid advertising campaigns to reach a broader audience.

8. Engage and Retain Users: Keep users engaged with regular updates, new features, and excellent customer support. Encourage user feedback and use it to improve your app. Implement push notifications to keep users informed and engaged.

9. Analyze Performance: Use analytics tools to track user behavior, app performance, and revenue. Analyze the data to identify areas for improvement and optimize your app for better user experience and higher earnings.

Let's walk through an example of creating a successful mobile app. Suppose you have an idea for a fitness app that provides personalized workout plans and tracks user progress. Here's a step-by-step approach:

1. Identify Your App Idea: Focus on creating a fitness app called "FitJourney" that offers customized workout routines and progress tracking.
2. Plan Your App: Outline features such as user profiles, workout plans, progress tracking, and community forums. Sketch wireframes and design the app's user interface.
3. Choose a Development Approach: Hire a freelance developer to build the app for both iOS and Android platforms.
4. Develop Your App: Work with the developer to create the app, ensuring it is user-friendly and visually appealing. Test the app thoroughly before launch.
5. Implement Monetization Strategies: Offer in-app purchases for premium workout plans and ad-free experience. Implement ads for free users.
6. Launch Your App: Publish "FitJourney" on the Apple App Store and Google Play Store. Create an engaging app description and use high-quality visuals.

7. Promote Your App: Promote "FitJourney" through social media, fitness influencers, and app review websites. Run targeted ads on Facebook and Instagram.

8. Engage and Retain Users: Regularly update the app with new workout plans and features. Use push notifications to keep users engaged and motivated.

9. Analyze Performance: Track user engagement, in-app purchases, and ad revenue using analytics tools. Use the data to improve the app and optimize monetization strategies.

TIPS FOR SUCCESS

❖ Focus on User Experience: Ensure your app is intuitive, visually appealing, and provides value to users.

❖ Stay Updated: Keep up with the latest trends and technologies in app development to ensure your app remains competitive.

❖ Collect and Act on Feedback: Listen to user feedback and continuously improve your app based on their suggestions.

❖ Invest in Marketing: Allocate resources to promote your app effectively and reach a wider audience.

❖ Monitor and Optimize: Regularly analyze app performance and revenue, and make necessary adjustments to maximize earnings..

CONCLUSION

Creating a mobile app is a dynamic and scalable way to generate passive income. By developing a high-quality app that meets user needs, implementing effective monetization strategies, and promoting it to a broad audience, you can build a sustainable income stream. Embrace the potential of mobile technology and turn your innovative ideas into a profitable venture that contributes to your financial independence and long-term success..

9.
ROBO-ADVISORS

Investing in the financial markets can be daunting, especially for those who lack the time or expertise to manage their portfolios actively. Robo-advisors offer a modern solution, using algorithms and technology to manage investments on your behalf. By leveraging robo-advisors, you can generate passive income with minimal effort, making it an attractive option for investors of all experience levels. This chapter will explore how robo-advisors work, their benefits, and how to get started.

- Robo-advisors are automated investment platforms that use algorithms to create and manage a diversified portfolio based on your financial goals, risk tolerance, and investment horizon. These platforms typically offer lower fees than traditional financial advisors and provide a hands-off approach to investing, making them ideal for generating passive income.

"UNLOCK EFFORTLESS INVESTING WITH ROBO-ADVISORS—AUTOMATE YOUR PORTFOLIO FOR STEADY PASSIVE INCOME AND FINANCIAL GROWTH."

BENEFITS OF ROBO-ADVISORS

1. Low Fees: Robo-advisors usually charge lower management fees compared to human financial advisors, allowing you to keep more of your investment returns.

2. Accessibility: With low minimum investment requirements, robo-advisors make it easy for anyone to start investing, regardless of their financial situation.

3. Diversification: Robo-advisors create diversified portfolios, reducing risk and enhancing the potential for steady returns.

4. Automatic Rebalancing: These platforms automatically rebalance your portfolio to maintain the desired asset allocation, ensuring your investments stay aligned with your goals.

5. Tax Efficiency: Many robo-advisors offer tax-loss harvesting, which can help minimize your tax liability and improve after-tax returns.

.

HOW TO GET STARTED

1. Choose a Robo-Advisor Platform: Research and compare different robo-advisor platforms to find one that suits your needs. Popular options include Betterment, Wealthfront, and Vanguard Digital Advisor. Consider factors such as fees, account minimums, investment options, and additional features.

2. Set Up Your Account: Once you've chosen a platform, sign up and create an account. You'll need to provide personal information, including your financial goals, risk tolerance, and investment horizon. The robo-advisor will use this information to design a customized investment plan.

3. Fund Your Account: Deposit funds into your robo-advisor account. Many platforms have low minimum investment requirements, making it easy to start with a small amount of capital.

4. Review Your Investment Plan: The robo-advisor will create a diversified portfolio tailored to your needs. Review the proposed investment plan to ensure it aligns with your financial goals and risk tolerance.

5. Monitor Performance: While robo-advisors handle the day-to-day management of your investments, it's essential to periodically review your account to stay informed about your portfolio's performance. Most platforms provide easy-to-use dashboards and regular updates.

6. Adjust as Needed: If your financial goals or risk tolerance change, update your information on the platform. The robo-advisor will adjust your portfolio accordingly to reflect your new preferences.

Let's walk through an example of generating passive income using a robo-advisor. Suppose you have $5,000 to invest and choose Betterment as your platform. Here's a step-by-step approach:

1. Choose a Robo-Advisor Platform: Select Betterment for its user-friendly interface, low fees, and comprehensive features.
2. Set Up Your Account: Sign up on Betterment's website and provide information about your financial goals, risk tolerance, and investment horizon.
3. Fund Your Account: Deposit $5,000 into your Betterment account.
4. Review Your Investment Plan: Betterment creates a diversified portfolio of ETFs tailored to your profile. Review and approve the plan.
5. Monitor Performance: Use Betterment's dashboard to track your portfolio's performance and receive regular updates.
6. Adjust as Needed: If your financial situation changes, update your preferences, and Betterment will adjust your portfolio to match your new goals.

TIPS FOR SUCCESS

❖ Start Early: The earlier you start investing, the more time your money has to grow. Even small amounts can compound significantly over time.
❖ Be Consistent: Regularly contribute to your robo-advisor account to take advantage of dollar-cost averaging, reducing the impact of market volatility.
❖ Stay Informed: While robo-advisors manage your investments, staying informed about market trends and economic factors can help you make better decisions.
❖ Reinvest Earnings: Reinvest dividends and interest earnings to maximize your portfolio's growth potential.

❖ Be Patient: Investing is a long-term strategy. Avoid reacting to short-term market fluctuations and focus on your long-term goals..

CONCLUSION

Robo-advisors provide a convenient and efficient way to generate passive income through automated investing. By leveraging technology to create and manage a diversified portfolio, robo-advisors offer a hands-off approach that can help you achieve your financial goals with minimal effort. Whether you're a novice investor or looking to simplify your investment strategy, robo-advisors can be a valuable tool in building a sustainable and growing passive income stream. Embrace the power of automated investing and take a significant step towards financial independence and long-term wealth creation.

10.
SELLING STOCK PHOTOS

I n the digital age, visual content is in high demand. From websites and blogs to marketing materials and social media posts, businesses and individuals constantly seek high-quality images to enhance their projects. Selling stock photos is an excellent way to generate passive income, leveraging your photography skills to create a continuous revenue stream. This chapter will guide you through the process of creating, uploading, and selling stock photos to earn passive income.Real estate crowdfunding involves multiple investors pooling their money to invest in real estate projects. These projects can range from residential properties to commercial real estate developments. By leveraging the collective funds of many investors, crowdfunding platforms can provide access to high-value properties that might be out of reach for individual investors.

- Stock photos are images that photographers license for specific uses. Buyers, such as businesses, marketers, and content creators, purchase these licenses to legally use the photos in their projects. Stock photo websites act as intermediaries, hosting the images and facilitating transactions between photographers and buyers."Unlock financial freedom by letting your money work for you through real estate crowdfunding—where collective investment meets effortless passive income."

BENEFITS OF SELLING STOCK PHOTOS

1. Passive Income: Once uploaded, stock photos can be sold multiple times, generating ongoing revenue without additional effort.
2. Global Market: Stock photo websites have a vast audience, allowing you to reach potential buyers worldwide.
3. Flexibility: You can shoot and upload photos at your own pace, making it a flexible side income stream.
4. Low Barrier to Entry: With basic photography equipment and some creativity, you can start selling stock photos with minimal initial investment.

HOW TO GET STARTED

1. Invest in Equipment: While you don't need the most expensive gear, having a good quality camera and basic photography equipment can significantly improve the quality of your photos. Consider investing in a DSLR or mirrorless camera, along with a few versatile lenses and essential accessories like tripods and lighting.

2. Learn the Basics of Photography: Understanding fundamental photography concepts such as composition, lighting, and exposure is crucial. There are many free and paid resources online, including tutorials, courses, and forums, where you can learn and improve your skills.

3. Identify Your Niche: Specializing in a specific type of photography can help you stand out. Popular niches include lifestyle, nature, business, food, travel, and technology. Choose a niche that interests you and has high demand.

4. Create High-Quality Photos: Focus on creating high-quality, high-resolution images that meet the standards of

stock photo websites. Pay attention to composition, lighting, and clarity. Edit your photos to enhance their visual appeal using software like Adobe Lightroom or Photoshop.

5. Research Stock Photo Websites: Choose reputable stock photo websites to upload and sell your images. Popular platforms include Shutterstock, Adobe Stock, iStock, and Getty Images. Each platform has different requirements and commission structures, so research and choose the ones that best fit your needs.

6. Set Up an Account: Create accounts on your chosen stock photo websites. This usually involves providing personal information and verifying your identity.

7. Upload Your Photos: Start uploading your photos to the platforms. Pay attention to each platform's submission guidelines, including file size, format, and metadata requirements. Properly keyword your images to improve discoverability.

8. Optimize Keywords and Descriptions: Use relevant keywords and descriptions to ensure your photos appear in search results. Think like a buyer and use terms that people might use to find images related to your photos.

9. Promote Your Portfolio: Share your stock photo portfolio on social media, your website, and photography forums to increase visibility and attract more buyers.

10. Monitor Sales and Trends: Regularly check your sales and analyze which types of images are performing well. Stay updated on market trends and adjust your photography to meet the evolving demands.

Let's walk through an example of generating passive income through stock photos. Suppose you have a passion for travel photography. Here's a step-by-step approach:

1. Invest in Equipment: Purchase a mid-range DSLR camera and a couple of versatile lenses.

2. Learn the Basics of Photography: Take online courses to improve your understanding of composition and lighting.

3. Identify Your Niche: Focus on travel photography, capturing landscapes, cityscapes, and cultural experiences.

4. Create High-Quality Photos: Travel to different locations and take high-resolution, visually appealing photos. Edit them to enhance their quality.

5. Research Stock Photo Websites: Choose Shutterstock, Adobe Stock, and iStock as your platforms.

6. Set Up an Account: Create accounts on these platforms and complete the verification process.

7. Upload Your Photos: Upload your travel photos, ensuring they meet the platforms' submission guidelines.

8. Optimize Keywords and Descriptions: Use keywords like "travel," "landscape," "cityscape," "adventure," and specific location names.

9. Promote Your Portfolio: Share your stock photo portfolio on Instagram, your travel blog, and photography forums.

10. Monitor Sales and Trends: Track which photos sell the most and adapt your photography style

TIPS FOR SUCCESS

❖ 1. Invest in Good Equipment: Ensure you have a decent camera and essential accessories like lenses, tripods, and lighting to produce high-quality images.

❖ 2. Master Photography Basics: Learn and practice key photography concepts such as composition, lighting, exposure, and editing to enhance your photos.

❖ 3. Find Your Niche: Specialize in a specific type of photography that interests you and is in demand, such as lifestyle, nature, business, or travel.

❖ 4. Create High-Quality Content: Focus on taking high-resolution, well-composed photos that meet the technical standards of stock photo websites.

❖ 5. Use Photo Editing Software: Edit your images using tools like Adobe Lightroom or Photoshop to enhance their visual appeal and correct any imperfections.

❖ 6. Research Stock Photo Platforms: Choose reputable stock photo websites like Shutterstock, Adobe Stock, iStock, and Getty Images, and understand their submission requirements and commission structures.

❖ 7. Optimize Keywords and Descriptions: Use relevant and specific keywords to describe your photos, making them easier to find in search results.

❖ 8. Upload Regularly: Consistently add new photos to keep your portfolio fresh and relevant, increasing the chances of making sales.

❖ 9. Stay Updated on Trends: Monitor current trends in photography and popular search terms to capture images that meet market demand.

❖ 10. Promote Your Portfolio: Share your stock photo portfolio on social media, personal websites, and photography forums to increase visibility and attract more buyers.

CONCLUSION

Real estate crowdfunding offers an accessible and effective way to generate passive income. By leveraging the power of collective investment, you can enjoy the benefits of real estate ownership without the associated hassles. With careful research and strategic investments, real estate crowdfunding can be a valuable addition to your passive income portfolio.